IMAGES OF ENGLAND

BRIGHOUSE
AND DISTRICT

LABORE ET PRUDENTIA

IMAGES OF ENGLAND

BRIGHOUSE
AND DISTRICT

CHRIS HELME

TEMPUS

Frontispiece: The Brighouse coat of arms. *'Labore et Prudentia'* means 'By Labour and Prudence'. The armorial bearings of the municipal borough of Brighouse were granted by Letters of Patent dated 28 March 1894. The arms were derived from the arms of the Brighouse and Rastrick families, who lived in the district in the seventeenth century. The golden lion and black crescents came from the Brighouse family arms, while the red roses are from the arms of the Rastrick family. It is interesting to note the inclusion of red roses on the coat of arms of a Yorkshire borough.

First published 2005

Tempus Publishing Limited
The Mill, Brimscombe Port,
Stroud, Gloucestershire, GL5 2QG
www.tempus-publishing.com

© Chris Helme, 2005

The right of Chris Helme to be identified as the Author
of this work has been asserted in accordance with the
Copyrights, Designs and Patents Act 1988.

British Library Cataloguing in Publication Data.
A catalogue record for this book is available from the British Library.

ISBN 0 7524 3577 9

Typesetting and origination by Tempus Publishing Limited.
Printed in Great Britain.

Contents

Acknowledgements

I have been involved in local history for almost thirty years and there have been many people who have helped me by sharing their memories and photographs, for which I will always be grateful. Some of those photographs have been included in this publication.

My own interest in local history has been encouraged by a number of people, but the weekly nostalgia and reminiscences contribution to the *Brighouse Echo* by the late Ralph Wade was probably one of my greatest inspirations. I was an avid fan of his column for many years, but little did I know that one day I would be asked to step into his shoes and take on the same role following his retirement in 1985.

Almost all of the photographs in this publication belong to me, but there are a few of them that have been kindly loaned by friends and contacts, and I would like to thank them for their support with this publication. These include: Mrs Gladys Wade, Peter Booth, Jeffrey Crawshaw, Roy Black, the *Brighouse Echo*, Ralph Howard, Peter Bates, Chris Freeman, David Carter, Gerald Hartley, John Brooke, Glyn Foster, Dorothy Stevens, Derek Hamer, Barbara Rice, Brian Laycock.

Copyright approval has been sought wherever necessary, but in certain cases copyright could not be traced. Even though, I would still like to thank all those unknown people.

And finally… I would like to give a special thanks to my wife Barbara for helping and supporting me with the preparation of this and all my previous publications, and for listening to my thoughts and occasional moans and groans as each one has progressed; and to Mum and Dad for the help and support they have given with proofreading the captions in this publication and many others previously.

Introduction

I remember in 1986 listening to people saying that the local aspect had gone out of Brighouse and its surrounding communities – now, almost twenty years on, I suppose it is even truer than it was then.

Some have said that community spirit is a bit old-fashioned and belongs to a bygone era. I hope that through the pages of this book I can take you on a journey through time and look back at some of the many aspects of Brighouse and its surrounding communities that you had forgotten, or maybe never even knew about. I will be showing you some of the things which have helped to shape this area. I have included many of the people who live and have lived here; in some cases people who may have been your relatives. These are the people who have worked here and helped to develop the town's prosperity, and make it what it is today.

We will look at transport and how it has changed people's lives; buildings (both public and private) and how they have changed; housing, and how for many people it developed from depressing rows of terraced backstreet properties to the new and modern social housing; and private housing, including the large estate mansions, their demise and the rise of the new homeowner. We will also look at the daily lives of local people and see how they helped to shape the industrial fortunes of the town. The Industrial Revolution and the Canal Age brought great changes to Brighouse, but it was the people of the town that helped to bring about those developments.

I am a firm believer that the more you know about the place in which you live, the more you will be able to appreciate it for what it is. If an opportunity presents itself we should grab it with both hands and help to make our community a better place.

Many of these photographs are being seen for the first time. If you have any comments or would like to add anything about the photographs I would be pleased to hear from you. This is not meant to be purely a history book, but also an insight, an opportunity of seeing over 200 captured moments in the life of Brighouse and its surrounding communities, and a few of the people who have and still do live there.

Chris Helme BEM
E-mail: chrishelme3539.brighouse@zen.co.uk

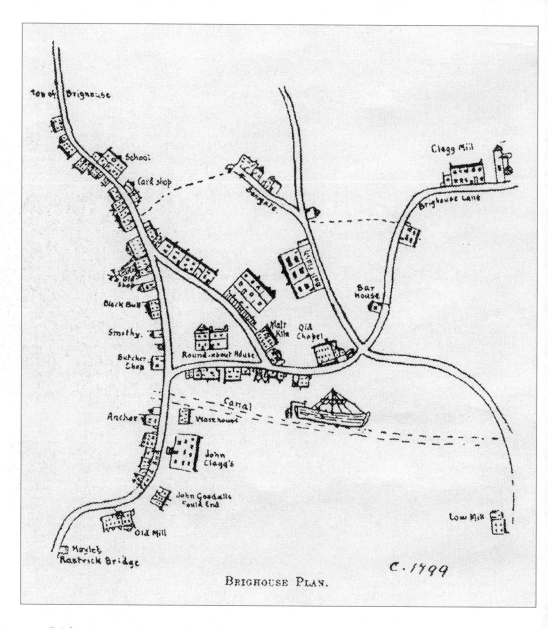

Brighouse town centre, *c.* 1799. Looking at this early drawing of the road network in the town centre, it is possible to work out where many of the present-day roads have developed from.

one

Brighouse

There have been many changes in the town centre, particularly over the last forty years, with one redevelopment after another. This was the day the town pump was demolished. It stood in what we now call Thornton Square; in 1912 it was between a triangular-shaped property called the Holroyd Buildings and the town hall. Sitting with his hand on the hammer ready to do the job is Jimmy Briggs, surrounded by the rest of the demolition gang.

The large building with the clock is the town hall, which was built in 1886 after a competition for architects. Following the demolition of the Holroyd Buildings in 1913 the vacant space was named Thornton Square. It was named after the incumbent mayor, Robert Thornton JP. In 1914 he was responsible for funding the new balustrade and the clock, which was nicknamed 'Ow'd Bob'.

Mayor Robert Thornton JP and his mayoress Mrs J. Atkinson (his niece) in their carriage, about to set off to another engagement. The carriage is standing outside the town hall in the cobbled road known as Union Street, which disappeared following the demolition of the Holroyd Buildings (the building to the left of the carriage) in 1913.

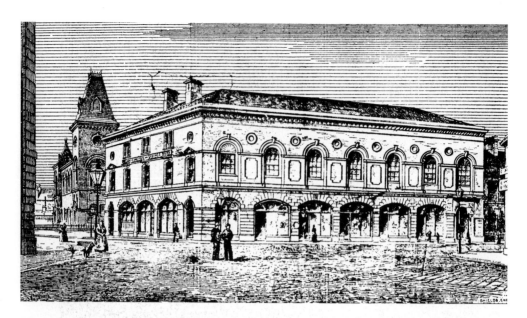

The Hipperholme–cum–Brighouse township was in existence for centuries, but in 1866 the formal separation took place. The new Brighouse Local Board (forerunner to the borough council) needed premises to run their administration, and these were built in 1866, owned by the Brighouse Town Hall Company and shared with eight ground-floor shops and the Brighouse Mechanics' Institute. A date stone can be seen just below the right-hand side roof guttering of the building.

The Manor House was the home of John Bottomley, a maltster who was one of the early entrepreneurs in the town. The house became the first bank to open in Brighouse when it was bought by the Halifax Commercial Bank. The Manor House was demolished in 1875; the building on its right-hand side was the old malt kiln, which had stood for almost 300 years when it too was demolished to make way for the new town hall in 1884.

William Smith was born in Greetland in 1839, and from the age of twelve he worked at the family business. Once he had established his own business he was actively involved with the Rastrick Local Board as the ratepayers' representative. Being a workaholic his health began to suffer, forcing early retirement. He returned to public life in the new borough council in 1893, and following the untimely death of the first-choice mayor, Frederick Laxton, he was elected as the town's first citizen. He is remembered for his generosity, having built the local art gallery, Rastrick library and the Smith orphanage.

This photograph, showing the bridge from Brighouse across the River Calder to Rastrick and looking towards Elland, was taken between 1895 and 1910 by a member of the Brighouse Photographic Society. This area of Brighouse is very low-lying and has always been susceptible to flooding. All the property on the right-hand side has since been demolished, in the interest of progress.

An 1884 panoramic view of Brighouse town centre, looking across from Lillands. It is interesting to note how many chimneys towered over the town all those years ago. Brighouse's industrial prosperity and diversity primarily developed alongside the two water courses (the River Calder and the Calder & Hebble Navigation Canal) during the Industrial Revolution.

The floods of September 1946, which many will remember – this is Lower Briggate, which has always suffered during the floods. In the distance are Thomas Sugden's flour mills, which had suffered many times from rising flood waters. The image of victims of the floods having to row themselves to safety was a common sight in this area. The property on the right is now part of a car park, and the cottages on the left were demolished to make way for the Thomas Sugden grain silos.

Wood Street, another part of Brighouse town centre which was caught in the deluge on Thursday 19 September 1946. While the young lad may have thought that it was good fun, the householders who are looking on would no doubt be hoping that the water does not get any deeper, and that the passing vehicles travel no faster, creating waves. Most of these terraced houses had cellars, and the minimum flooding occupants could expect was their cellar being flooded out, yet again.

The Thomas Sugden Flour Mills Company was started in Brighouse in 1828, and over the years it employed many local families. In the 1960s a number of memorable events took place. For example, in July 1961 a remarkable feat of construction took place when another storey was added to the Brighouse mills, raising their height by a further seven metres. Also, on Wednesday 9 October 1963, a six-storey grain warehouse caught fire. Here we see the builders working alongside the canal on the new development work at the mills.

The Canal Age arrived in Brighouse in 1757, but a little over two hundred years later the day of the working barge was coming to an end. These days the canal is used more for leisure purposes, including water buses, canal festivals and fun days. Taken on 1 October 1984, this photograph shows one of those happy and entertaining days, with a young man entertaining a large audience.

It is rare to see the canal frozen over – the last time it was frozen for weeks on end was all the way back in 1834. Here we see the canal on Boxing Day 1981, when the ice was still thick and not even the brick thrown in could puncture the icy surface.

Blakeborough's Bridge, as it is commonly known, was for many years a very useful link from one side of the Ward river to the other. This photograph was taken on Monday 15 February 1962, when the workmen were still at an early stage of its construction. Sadly, for many years it has been closed off in the interests of safety; extensive maintenance work is needed, and as yet no-one has been able to sanction the six-figure cost needed to bring the bridge up to modern safety standards.

This is probably the earliest known photograph of the first railway station at Brighouse. It was opened on Monday 5 October 1840, with the first train arriving promptly at 10 a.m. This station was opened even before Bradford had their railway station. However, in August 1872 it was closed down and a new station was opened on the opposite side of the road, with the old one being converted into a goods station. On 3 January 1970 the newer station was also closed. Brighouse remained without a railway station until the present one was officially opened on 29 May 2000.

Here is a happy crowd – all ready to leave on holiday from Brighouse railway station. As was often the custom in those days everyone went in their best clothes and top coat, whether it was summer or winter.

Thomas Sugden was born in Bradford in 1796. In 1818 he moved to Brighouse and opened his own business as a grocer at the bottom of Parsonage Lane. In 1829 (at the age of thirty-three) he became a miller, and his flour business flourished well into the twentieth century.

Richard Kershaw was born in 1832 in Wyke, and his family moved to The Crescent in Brighouse the following year. He married Sophia Baines (right), the daughter of another local entrepreneur, and in 1864 he gave up the life of a greengrocer and went into the silk industry. The culmination of his business was to buy part of the Wellholme estate and commission local architect George Hepworth to build the Woodvale silk mill, the largest mill building in Brighouse at that time, which was completed in 1881. At one time it employed as many as 700 people, but sadly the mill burned down in December 1985.

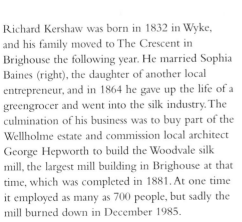

Henry Lockwood was the licensee at the George Hotel from 1879 to 1893, and his name on the sign is the only clue to the approximate age of this photograph. These premises became an important landmark in February 1904, when the first tramcar from Halifax arrived on the new extended route from Stump Cross down into Brighouse; the terminus of this new route was at the George Hotel.

Opposite above: During the 1870s new mills were being built at a rate previously unseen. Without doubt one of the grandest buildings at this time was the Ormerod Bros' new Alexandra Mill, which was built in Millroyd Street in 1872 to house their silk-spinning business. The foundation stone was laid on 13 September 1871 by local architect George Hepworth. For over thirty years this mill employed over 400 people, often including whole families.

Opposite below: On 26 October 1903 the Alexandra Mill, which at that time was still referred to by many employees as the 'new mill', broke for dinner at the usual time. With just a few minutes left before everyone was due to return to work, the chatter amongst workmates was shattered by the ear-piercing sound of the fire alarm. Not even six fire brigades could bring the fire under control. The mill was completely gutted (at an estimated loss of £40,000), leaving 400 people without work.

Throughout the history of any community there are periods of town centre redevelopment (or, to use the 'buzz' word of the moment, regeneration). These nineteenth-century properties are Nos 14-20 Park Street, opposite the post office, and were photographed in 1929 just prior to their demolition. Today this remains an open space, used by the Eurocar Car Audio & Security Company; the building in the distance is the Salvation Army citadel.

In more recent times further redevelopment has taken place throughout Brighouse. During the 1950s and '60s many more of the town's nineteenth-century houses were demolished. These properties at the end of Elland Road were demolished as part of another phase of regeneration. Many of the displaced families were re-housed in new social housing estates, at either Field Lane in Rastrick or Stoney Lane in Lightcliffe.

Slead Syke at the turn of the nineteenth century looked very different from how it does today. The tall buildings on the right-hand side were demolished during the 1930s and the property on the left-hand side made way for new semi-detached houses at the bottom of Halifax Road. The only property in this photograph still remaining is the row of cottages at the bottom of Halifax Road, which today stands at the junction with Granny Hall Lane.

A winter scene on Halifax Road during the mid–1950s. It is a rare event to see snow this deep nowadays, another sign of the times perhaps. Many town centre workers would have called at the newsagents on the left when it was owned by Mrs Backhouse. All that property was swept aside in the interests of progress during the 1960s, and eventually this area became part of the new town centre bypass in the early 1970s. All that remains is the Bethel church on the right, which has stood since 1907. Today it is the home of the Central Methodist church.

Above: Looking back at housing in the old borough involves looking at the days when the shopkeeper and his family always lived over their shop. This photograph was taken in around 1890 and shows the Commercial Street provisions shop of George Day, who lived above with his wife Hannah and their family. Where was this shop in Commercial Street? Today it is No.82, which is the business premises of Czerwik's cheese and wine shop.

Above: The Brighouse Wheelers on one of their summer outings *c.* 1908. A cycling club was first formed in 1884, and this became a popular pastime very quickly. One of the greatest local cycling exponents was James Joy. The club first met in the Cocoa House Tavern, and at the inaugural meeting it had nineteen members on its books. However, the following year they moved to the Royal Hotel. The cyclists held regular runs for eight or nine months of each year.

Right: In this 1920s photograph, the building on the left is the Black Swan Hotel in Lower Briggate. Its name can be clearly seen on its signage. Mind you, I am sure many readers will recall the days when it was simply known as the 'Mucky Duck'. A trade directory of 1895 describes it as '… another commodious set of premises visited regularly for almost two hundred years by commercial travellers, country gentlemen and farmers'. Owing to a structural fault in the roof, one storey was later removed.

Opposite below: Arthur Webster's leather shop, in around 1906. Back in those days the shop was situated at No. 31 Bethel Street, on the corner with Canal Street. In the trade directory of that year Webster was described as a saddler and maker of portmanteaus (a French word for a large leather suitcase that opens into two hinged compartments). Judging from the number he has on display in his front window there are plenty for his more discerning customers to choose from. What is probably his workshop on the right also has a varied choice of horse collars and other related goods on display.

A small number of companies have stood the test of time in and around Brighouse. One of those which is still (after seventy-five years) offering a first class service is J.C. Bates & Sons Ltd, one of the few traditional family-run businesses in the town.

This scene from around 1910 shows what was often referred to as a 'double header' – two trams together outside the tramcar terminus at the George Hotel. Gone are the days of the old trams, and gone are the days when the town centre 'Bobby' would leave his cape hung on a nail on the corner of the George while he carried out point duty and then walked his town centre beat for a hour or so, with the full knowledge that his cape would still be both where he left it and intact.

The Bow Window – for those readers not old enough to remember it, this establishment was considered to be a Brighouse institution. It could certainly be said that it was Brighouse's first 'takeaway'. The business was started in 1864 in Huddersfield Road, but it will always be associated with No. 72 Briggate and of course the time it was owned by the Stake Brothers. How many of you can almost still taste the finest sausages, pies and muffins? Customers would travel from far and wide to feast on the delights of the Bow Window whilst it was open, every night between 5.30 p.m. and 11 p.m.

This was a comic advertisement which the proprietors Helliwell and Harry Stake used to great effect. It would probably draw serious criticism these days but in its time it reflected the success of their business. Whatever people think of it today doesn't really matter because all those generations who visited what was a real institution in Brighouse would never hear a wrong word said against it. Edmund Stake, Helliwell's son, decided in October 1959 that time was catching up with him, and so it was time to call it a day.

Commercial Street, the main shopping thoroughfare in Brighouse town centre. It conjures up memories of many well-known shops and businesses, both past and present. This photograph was taken during the 1960s, when the town centre was buzzing with shoppers all looking out for the latest bargain. On-street parking appears to have been as much a problem then as it is today.

Bradford Road in 1904. The building with the balcony was the old Liberal club, where in May 1882 the local industrialists met and demanded to see Inspector Hey, the local police chief. This was during the so-called 'Irish Riots' in the town centre, which occurred following the assassination of Lord Frederick Cavendish in Phoenix Park, Dublin. Local Liberal MP Lord Cavendish visited Brighouse many times and was well-thought-of. Wrongly, the indigenous population took their anger out on the local Irish labourers who, far from being troublemakers, were very hard-working and industrious people.

Galas, carnivals and parades are not a new phenomenon; they have been part of life in local communities for centuries, and Brighouse is no exception. The first such events were the pig fairs of the mid-nineteenth century, followed by the various flower and animal shows and hospital charity events, right through to today's Brighouse charity gala. These events re-invigorate community spirit, although they are considered to be old-fashioned by many these days. Seen here in this 1920s Commercial Street scene is one of the annual (and very successful) demonstration parades.

Above: The foundation stone of the new Brighouse parish church of St Martin was laid on 22 March 1830, and the building was completed on 10 February 1831. Its consecration was performed by the Archbishop of York, Dr Vernon Harcourt. Brighouse was at that time in the diocese of York (the dioceses of Wakefield and Ripon had not yet come into existence). A grant was awarded from the 'Million Churches Fund' towards the building of the church, in addition to numerous other private contributions.

Left: The church's centenary celebrations took place in 1931 with a culmination of events in November, each day in the week having a theme of its own. For example, one day it was missionary work, another day the work of the day schools. This large cake was baked to celebrate this memorable and important milestone in the history of Brighouse.

The split of Methodism into two parts saw the New Connexion chapel at Bethel being built in 1811. Its followers had left the old Methodist church at Park Chapel, which had been opened in 1795. This photograph shows the frontage of the old Bethel chapel in Bethel Street. One of the former ministers at the chapel was General William Booth, who went on to found the Salvation Army.

In 1795 a Clifton farmer bought a plot of land in Bethel Street for £47, and it was here that the first Park chapel was built. In 1875 plans for a new chapel in a 'Romanesque' Italian style were submitted and passed. The last service in the old chapel was on 5 July 1876, and the first service in the new chapel took place on 27 June 1878. Today it has been confined to the history books as a place of worship, but the chapel building remains and is now a J.D. Wetherspoon pub, 'The Richard Ostler'.

The local church or chapel was not only a place of worship, taking care of people's spiritual needs, it also took care of the congregation's social needs as well. These children were taking part in the Park Diamond Jubilee celebrations on 5 July 1938, and included: Mabel Radley and Stanley Wardingley; Nora Sutcliffe and Cyril Hill; Irene Hardcastle and Walter Vickerman; Margaret Preston and John Gregory; Nancy Lancaster and Walter Austwick; Rhoda Knight and John Whittingham; Ada Brook and Gordon Taylor; Jean Mitchell and Arnold Brooke; Dorothy Drake (pianist) and Muriel Cogan; Irene Goldspink; Margaret Chapman, and Marjorie Westmorland.

Above: Party for the ladies of the lodge. This occasion was during the 1950s, when the Clifton Masonic Lodge held their 'Ladies Evening' at the Assembly Rooms in Briggate. The group includes Fred Lapish, George Stillingfleet, Sir Herbert Redfearn, George Balmforth, Arthur Reeve, Norman Brooke, Norman Lockwood, Wilf Crew, Harry Marsden and John Albert Hallowell, and of course their wives and guests.

Left: Samuel Baines (born in 1814) bought two and a half acres of land from the Noble family. On this land he developed his Victoria Mills complex, or Baines Square as everyone knew it. He introduced the first fire engine to Brighouse with his private Victoria Mills fire volunteers, and his engine *Neptune*. Like his father he was an industrial pioneer, and was largely responsible for helping to spread the name of Brighouse far and wide. He died on 25 July 1866. Today the site is occupied by a Sainsbury's supermarket.

Brighouse's police force in 1884. This was taken two years after the so-called 'Irish Riots' in Brighouse, which followed the assassination of Lord Frederick Cavendish, the former Liberal MP, in Phoenix Park, Dublin. His constituency had included Brighouse. Police officers on parade include, from left to right, back row: -?-, PC Calvert, PC Johnson, PC Jenkins, PC Riach, PC Bayliss. Front row: PC Dixon, Sgt Ramm, Inspector Hey (in plain clothes), Sgt Drake, PC Barker, PC Beaumont. Sitting in the front: PC Greaves, PC Gill.

The earliest police station in Brighouse was the 'old lock-up' known as the 'Towser' on Elland Road. However, as the population of the town grew so did the need for a new modern police station. As the number of local police officers had grown to four by 1863, it was felt the need was urgent. This new police station was opened in what became known as Police Street (now Lawson Road) in 1865, and was to be used until it too became outdated and the present police station was opened in 1964. Here it is with wartime precautions in 1940.

Above: In spite of the risk from fire to the large textile mills, the earliest local firefighting facility had only been on a voluntary basis. With such an inadequate service and great demand from the public, the new borough council decided to create a new fire brigade. This new brigade was formed in 1897, with most of the firefighters recruited from the old volunteers. With their new Superintendent and steam-driven fire engine, the firefighters proudly posed for this photograph.

Left: The fire at Ormerod Bros in Alexander Mill on Monday 26 October 1903 brought home the harsh realities of being a firefighter. The engine was hurriedly prepared at the fire station and speedily made its way to the fire. Alexander Carmichael, one of the oldest and most respected of Brighouse's firefighters, was on board the appliance on that day. Hurtling through the town centre, he was thrown from the fire engine as one of its wheels hit a raised road sett. Such was the impact of his fall that he was killed instantly.

Left: The business premises of Joseph Lawson were at 19 Commercial Street at the turn of the nineteenth century. He took on the plumbing and glazing business of Henry Welsman in 1864. As the years went by, the business expanded and diversified into ironmongery, baths, gas fittings, chandeliers, cisterns and pipes. His showroom was a veritable Aladdin's cave. He was also an agent for Bissell's Carpet Sweepers, and for many other household names of the time. In later years he also had a shop in Ilkley.

Below: Whilst this invoice from Joseph Lawson's to local solicitor John Ayrton is dated 31 December 1917, it shows a new address from where the original shop was opened; it had moved to 68 & 70 Commercial Street. Note the decorative style of printing, and in particular the shop front illustration where the people are very small compared to the shop window they are looking through.

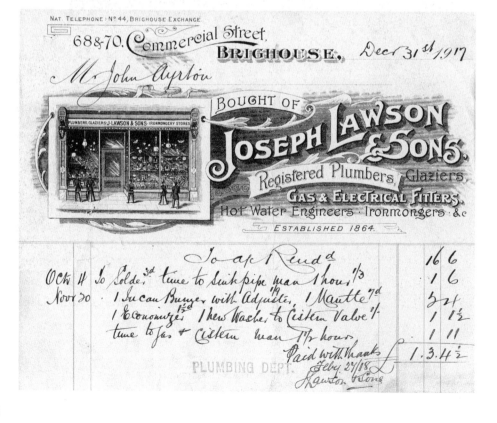

Taken during the 1960s, this view of Commercial Street shows the outfitters Burras Peake and Popley's. These premises are in what was originally Joseph Lawson's plumbers and glaziers. It is interesting to note the illuminated shop next door, which is Hillards Freezer Food Centre. Most Brighouse readers will tend to remember Hillards from the 1960s, but John Wesley Hillard had a store at No. 36 Briggate as early as 1906.

Blakeborough Valves was part of the Brighouse industrial scene for over 150 years. While Robert Blakeborough began experimenting with valves in his town centre cellar, it was his company's eventual expansion and move to what became known as their Woodhouse works that was to enable him to employ local people for generations. An interesting feature of this pre-1939 aerial view is the number of tall chimney stacks in the town centre.

This impressive Victorian house was called Brooklands, and was the home of Dr William and Ethel Skeels. On the 4 December 1936 plans were submitted by the Regal Cinema (Moldgreen) Ltd to build a new cinema on the site.

During the early years of the cinema in the Brighouse area there had been the Theatre-de-Luxe at Hipperholme, and small films were also shown at the old Empire theatre in Atlas Mill Lane. There was also a 'walk-in-movie' at Wellholme Park for a short while. However, it was the Albert and the Savoy which reigned supreme, until 1937, when the first purpose-built cinema (the Ritz) was opened on the site of Brooklands.

The business premises of John Pearson Nelson were at No. 19 Briggate. He was a cooper and cask dealer, and had been in business from as early as 1906 on this site. This corner of Brighouse was also the home of Barber's pie, peas and sausage shop, and a tripe restaurant, of all things, as well as Lister Kershaw the nurseryman and seedsman, and Louis Kershaw the wringing machine repairer and dealer. In more recent times it has been occupied by Hillards and a Tesco supermarket, and is presently the home of Wilkinson's.

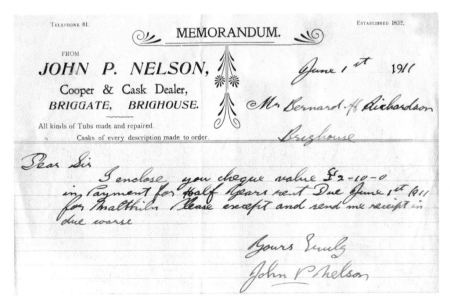

The document is what is described as a memorandum from John Pearson Nelson to his near neighbour, local solicitor Bernard H. Richardson (who in his spare time was also the secretary of the Brighouse Rangers). This document is a note regarding the £2 10s 0d (£2.50) John Nelson owed for half a year's rent, and is dated 1 June 1911. This document would suggest that Mr Richardson was probably the solicitor acting on behalf of the property's landlord.

Left: Mrs Susan Sunderland (*née* Sykes), who was born on 30 April 1819, lived at Spring Gardens, near Garden Road. She was initially trained as a soprano soloist by John Denham and Luke Settle (the local blacksmith), and later by Dan Sugden of Halifax. It is widely recognised that her first public performance was in September 1833 at Lightcliffe (old) church, making her debut at a musical benefit oratorio for the widow and family of Robert Sladden of Hipperholme. It was at this concert (when she was fourteen years old) that she was described at the 'Prima Donna of the North'.

Below: During the celebrations for her golden wedding anniversary in June 1888 she suggested that from the funds raised a music festival should be organised to take place in Huddersfield. Today the Mrs Sunderland music festival is more popular than ever. She died on 7 May 1905, and her funeral procession was watched by the largest gathering for any funeral in Brighouse that anyone could remember.

11 January 1956 – this was the first 'Teenagers' Civic Ball', held at the Waring Green community centre. It was reported at the time that this was a night when anything (unpleasant) could have happened – but didn't. With no rock and roll music it was left to the calmer tones of the New Embassy Orchestra to ensure everyone had a good evening. Attending along with the mayor Alderman Harry Edwards and his wife Eliza (right) were deputy mayor Leslie Hulme and his wife Joyce (left) and 200 teenagers. The MC's for the evening were Philip Helme and Joyce Waddington.

The final gathering of the former chief and senior officers of the council was at the Black Bull on 2 December 1975. From left to right, back row: Barry Parker (assistant housing manager), Gerry Norrie (deputy town clerk), Gordon Denham (acting deputy borough treasurer), Willie Jennings (public health officer), Bob Milner (cemetery superintendent), Dr Brock (medical officer), Brian Berry (deputy borough treasurer), Frank Clayton (housing manager), John Jepson (deputy librarian), Ian Leach (deputy borough engineer). Seated: Clifford Bland (borough engineer), David Young (borough treasurer), John Liddle (town clerk), Jim Bailey (chief librarian).

Joseph Fillingham was only twenty years old when he started what was to become a truly family-run butchers business at the top of Brighouse in 1848. After ten years he had built up such a sound business that he felt confident enough to move into the town centre at No. 26 Bethel Street. In 1883 he was joined by his son Sam, who took over the business following his father's death in 1903. Sam Fillingham was a shy, retiring man who was a long-standing member of the Brighouse Butchers Association - he died on 13 January 1920.

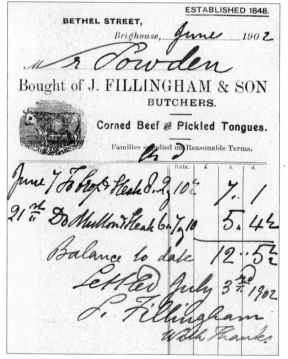

Left: This invoice from Sam Fillingham to a Mr Sowden is dated June 1902 and was paid on 3 July, and gives a fascinating insight into meat prices at the time.

Opposite below: Market Street in around 1940. This photograph was taken during a civil defence parade through the town centre, which was making its way to the old market site in Market Street. It is interesting to note the Stylo shoe shop (now Lords' Photographers) at the rear, and the protruding sign on the left for Ed Taylor's hairdressers – a familiar name in Brighouse even today.

Above: Nursing Sister Annie Wheatley (sitting in the front row on the left) is the only female named on the Brighouse war memorial. She was born in Brighouse, but in 1895 she moved to Birmingham to train as a nurse. In 1917 she was asked to go overseas on active service. Her ship left Bristol en route for Salonica, but was torpedoed and sank. She was commended by the Matron-in-Chief of the Territorial Forces Nursing Service for her bravery and coolness after the ship was sunk. Later she suffered a serious bout of bronchitis, and with her health failing she died on 1 August 1919, and was interred in Brighouse Cemetery.

Victory in Europe (VE) Day was Tuesday 8 May 1945, but it was marked in Brighouse five days later with a procession from the town hall to Wellholme Park for a thanksgiving service followed by a march pass outside the Ritz cinema. The salute was taken by the mayor Alderman J.V.F. Bottomley and Mrs Bottomley, and the senior military officer for the area Colonel R.H. Goldthorpe.

Thornton Square on 19 July 1919. This event saw the largest gathering ever assembled in the town centre. It was to celebrate the end of the First World War. The music was performed by the Brighouse & Rastrick Temperance Band. The macebearer is leading out the mayoral party to the temporary bandstand and rostrum. It was an occasion when the children of the borough led the parade into Thornton Square.

The Royal British Legion was revived after the Second World War and saw the Brighouse, Hipperholme and Southowram branches build their own headquarters in Bradford Road, next to J.C. Bates' garage. This is the big day when it was formally opened by the Earl of Scarborough in 1957. Today the premises are no longer owned or used by the Royal British Legion, and are the home of a private company.

Posing for the camera in Lawson Road during the 1980s are some of the veterans and stalwarts of the local Royal British Legion branches. Perhaps one of these gentlemen is your relative – some of those on parade include Frank Waddington, Edgar Clay, Harry Haldenby and Charles Hoare, to name but a few. Sadly most are no longer with us. It was from this meeting place on Lawson Road that they would set off on their regularly held daytrips and outings.

Brighouse Co-operative Society opened in 1856 and, while there were many changes over the years, there were none greater than when it became part of the Bradford Sunwin House Group in the late 1970s. Another change that made a significant difference was in 1957, when they opened the new self-service food hall in King Street. Self-service is commonplace today, but it wasn't in those days. Some may also remember that above this new building was the New Kingsway restaurant. The bunting is up to celebrate its grand opening.

Brighouse Co-operative Society's men's outfitting department was at the junction of King Street and Bradford Road, and had received a makeover in 1955. Once again this new department was run entirely on a self-service basis. On the first floor were the ready-made and bespoke tailoring sections, and tucked out of the view of the public were the tailoring workshop and fitting rooms. Throughout the 1960s and early 1970s some memorable staff included Clifford Sutcliffe, John Jolly, Ronald Cottington and Barbara Thorp, while Jack Bray occupied downstairs. Today this shop is a branch of Mackay's clothing store.

These properties are thought to have dated back to Queen Anne's reign (1702–1714). The history books tell us that during the English Civil War soldiers picketed these buildings, so it is likely that they were almost a hundred years older. The properties were aptly named Queen Anne's Square, but other than it being named after the Queen herself there is no historical evidence to show how the area got its name, who built it or who lived there.

In 1905 the Queen Anne's Square properties were in a poor state of repair and considered dangerous. Local architects were invited by the local Freemasons to submit plans for their new premises and a new borough club. The plans that were finally accepted were those by E.C. Brooke, who had offices in Huddersfield. The completed building was designed to fit between the Anchor Inn and the Bow Window. The new Assembly Rooms were officially opened on 17 July 1906.

Sykes' furniture shop at the corner of Mill Lane and Police Street (now Lawson Road), in a photograph taken around 1914. During the 1960s it was Kershaw's antiques shop, but like many areas in the town centre the building was swept away as part of the early 1970s redevelopments.

This is the corner of Park Street and Commercial Street during the 1930s, just prior to being demolished. This property had originally been built on the site of Zingo Nick, which was an area that housed many Irishmen who worked in the local quarries. Once this property had been demolished the new Burton men's outfitters shop and a billiard hall were built on the site. In later years it became the YEB showrooms, and is now the offices of the local Abbey Bank.

Once again we are looking along Commercial Street during the town centre redevelopments of the 1930s. All this property was demolished and replaced with new shop premises, many of which were to become familiar high street names, all equipped for the modern and discerning shopper of the 1930s. It was the tall building which was replaced by the new Burton shop, and the shop beyond (on the corner of Park Street) is a travel agent's shop today.

Coombes' shoe repairs at the corner of Bethel Street and Park Street during the late 1960s, followed by the Coffee Tavern and Joan's Bargain Stores. The last shop window before the old Bethel New Connexion chapel is the Brighouse Echo's front window. In those days, photographs displayed in the window each week would have individuals marked and highlighted with a circle or a triangle. Those people who were lucky enough to be highlighted won either 2s 6d or 5s.

Bowling has been a popular pastime for over a century in the Brighouse area. One of the first bowling greens was in Swan Field near the Black Swan public house in around 1840, with others following at Clifton in 1875, Rastrick Bowling Green Co. Ltd in 1902, Hove Edge in 1907, the Royal Oak at Lower Edge in 1908 and Woodlands on Birds Royd in 1910. Whilst a number of greens have disappeared, the popularity of bowls has hardly diminished. This is the Albion Bowling Club at Lane Head in around 1899.

Blakeborough Valves employed generations of local people throughout its long history. The laboratory department was just one of the departments which contributed to the company's success. In 1950 the staff included, from left to right, back row: Bob Lindsey, Jack Kershaw, Roger Blakeborough, Frank Slater, Albert Clegg, Gordon Foster, Fred Dale. Front row: Myra Lazenby; Alma Lazenby, Christine Bottomley.

A Victorian parlour in 1899. This was the home of Joseph Barber, who was the founder of the firm of solicitors Barber & Jessop in Church Lane. Note the mantle cover with the tasselled fringe, the small bamboo table and, of course, the obligatory accessory for all Victorian homes – the aspidistra plant. Then there is the marble fireplace and what we would refer to these days as 'Victorian bric-a-brac'. Just think of all that dusting!

PAPER SAVED MEANS MONEY SAVED.
HAND TO THE DUSTMAN
YOUR CLEAN WASTE PAPER.

Originally Atlas Mill Road refuse works was opened in August 1926. In 1933 the council entered into a contract with Thames Board Mills in Essex. To encourage householders to save waste paper the council distributed leaflets telling ratepayers how much the waste paper was helping the council's finances. In 1951 the council spent £6,537 on a new waste paper recovery building, plant and a new approach road. Once the site was in full operation it was one of the old borough council's success stories.

Garden Road – now, where did that road get its name from? It is difficult to imagine today that this tree-lined street is Garden Road, looking from Halifax Road towards the junction with Blackburn Road that we know today. This photograph was taken before the modern semis were built, and the high wall was clearly built to ensure the owner's privacy, but what was there to hide? A secret garden, perhaps?

Taking a peep over the wall from Garden Road, this is what you would have seen. The house was the former home of the Sugden family (local flour mill owners) and later the Ramsden family, and those not having seen it previously will agree that it is clear what was meant when local people referred to it as 'the big house'. The house was demolished in the late 1930s, with the houses in Garden Road, Blackburn Road and the 'Ye Farre Close' cul-de-sac being built on the site.

Right: George Stillingfleet will be remembered in Brighouse for a number of reasons, but principally as the mayor and a businessman. He was born in Sheffield, but once he had moved to Brighouse in 1933 he formed the company Home Wireless Service (Brighouse) Ltd with a group of colleagues, with him being appointed the managing director. The business traded under the name of Stillingfleet & Harper. In 1935 he was elected to the borough council. He became the sole owner of the company in 1950, which was also the year he was elected mayor. This is his shop in Commercial Street.

Below: In 1901 the old Bethel chapel was put up for sale – some land had been purchased at the bottom of Halifax Road for the new chapel some fifteen years earlier. On 2 March 1907 the new Bethel chapel was officially opened in the presence of a very large gathering, including the mayor of Brighouse Alderman William Smith JP, and a ceremony was carried out by the daughter of the lord mayor of Leeds, as her father was ill.

Woodhouse & Mitchell's workshop. In 1867 this company began as engineers and iron founders in Birds Royd, but in 1872 they relocated to larger premises at Clifton Bridge ironworks. They began making engines for many of the leading industrial companies, as well as the War Department. Two of their leading engines were the 'Compound Tandem Steam Engine' and the 'Compound Side by Side Engine'. By 1895 they had also diversified into manufacturing a wooden school desk with a metal frame. This was one of Brighouse's leading companies for many years.

Gone are the days of Percy Garside and Bob Davison and their Dales charabanc trips and mystery outings, where everyone knew even before they set off where they were going but only spoke about it in whispers in case the driver heard them. Invariably it meant an outing to Bolton Abbey and then fish and chips at Harry Ramsden's on the way back. This old Crossley charabanc is being driven by Bob Davison on a ladies' trip back in 1925.

T.A. Fox, a commercial stationer, bookseller and newsagent. This is a receipt from Tom Fox to a Mr G.S. Sowden, dated 16 September 1904, for a death announcement which appeared in the *Yorkshire Post* twice, *Evening Post* once and both the *Brighouse News* and *Brighouse Echo*. The announcement cost 12s 6d (62½p), with an additional 6d (2½p) for sending the notice by both telephone and tram.

Tom Fox is seen here standing inside the doorway to his shop. It is 25 December 1900 and this photograph was a gift to Mr and Mrs Charlie Jessop from George Hepworth, a local architect and one of the founder members of the Brighouse Photographic Society. The actual photograph was obviously taken long before 1900 as the shop stands next to the old malt kiln, which was demolished in 1884 to make way for the new town hall.

Community events have been a feature of Brighouse and its surrounding districts for almost two centuries. Here is a memorable moment from one of them, a crowning glory for one young lady – Judith Powell was crowned the 'Road Safety Queen' for 1956/57 by the mayoress Mrs Edwards on the Lane Head recreation ground, replacing out-going queen Patricia France. Judith's full retinue on the day included Jeremy Aske, Ian Marshall, Patricia Helliwell, Anne Peaker, Margaret Watling, Margaret Airey, Janice Berry and Marilyn Brooks.

Throughout those post-war years community spirit was at its peak. It seemed that a week never went by without one of the local organisations holding an event where members, friends and neighbours could meet and share a half-day together. This gathering in around 1952 was part of the Christmas celebrations at the Brighouse Labour Club.

Whiteley's Corner and their clock was a focal point for more years than most could remember. Situated at the corner of Bradford Road and Bethel Street, theirs was a thriving newsagents and tobacconists for years. The pedestrian crossing was installed at this location due to the huge numbers of workers pouring out of Birds Royd Lane and down into the town centre, a good reason why Lloyd's Bank opened a branch opposite Whiteley's in 1875. However, this has since been replaced by a Sainsbury's supermarket.

It was at that same time that John Wesley Hillard had his thriving grocers shop in Briggate. It was hardly surprising that it was also in Briggate that the new Hillards supermarket should be developed and opened in the early 1970s. Many local people were sceptical about opening Hillards at that end of town, believing that it would create a problem if shopping was concentrated at either end of the town centre (the Brighouse Cooperative Society were on the opposite side of Brighouse), leaving the smaller traders to struggle in the middle ground.

Throughout the 1970s the town centre went through yet another period of redevelopment. The bypass was considered by many to be a waste of money, but can you imagine the town centre traffic situation today without it? Many old established businesses were swept away, along with many of the old back streets of terraced houses, all in the name of progress; the town was now moving into a period of great change.

One of the most notable buildings to be swept aside for the new bypass was the Oddfellows Hall, seen here in 1970. Opened in 1850, it was the town's first public hall. Mrs Susan Sunderland performed many times here, and the Salvation Army visited here in the early 1880s, only to be encouraged to leave the town. During the twentieth century it was the replacement venue for rained-off open air film shows and band concerts in Wellholme Park. For many years it was also the rehearsal rooms of the Brighouse & Rastrick Band.

The Astoria Ballroom opened in February 1945, and Mayor John V.F. Bottomley CBE JP held a 'Victory in Europe Ball' in July of that year. In 1950 an informal application was received from Brighouse Motors Ltd about turning it into a garage and motor showroom. An informal enquiry also came in 1951 from Alexandre Ltd (Leeds). In 1956 Tommy Joy and Messrs Trews submitted a planning application for a change of use from a ballroom to retail premises. In July 1971 it was demolished, along with many other parts of the town centre.

For generations of families Clayton's Central Mart was the most popular shop in Brighouse. This town centre emporium sold everything from drapery to furnishings. Mr Clayton was continually moving to bigger and bigger premises, and even took on a warehouse in Nettleton's Yard. He had shops in both Commercial Street and Briggate with a telephone link between them, even though it was no more than a two minute walk. The end came in 1950 when his last remaining shop, in Briggate, was demolished.

Left: In 1906 the family grocery business of D. Powell & Son was at 44 Briggate, between Barnett Bros (where the public toilets are today) and the Black Bull in Thornton Square. This shopping list is dated 31 July 1902, when all of these items were bought by a Mr Sowden for 17s 6d (approximately 87p today).

Below: The large imposing double-fronted shop obviously had a wide and diverse choice for the discerning Brighouse housewife and shopper.

Right: The building in front of the church is the Sun Dial Inn, and which was one of the properties that was attacked and wrecked during the 'Irish Riots' of 1882. It was believed that secret meetings were held at the inn by members of the local Irish community – a belief that had no basis of truth to it. The property was previously the Mary Bedford charity school; its headmaster was Mr Isaac Heaton, who was at the school for almost fifty years. It was later demolished and for many years it was the site of the floral clock, but today the site forms part of a road and a car park.

Below: Judging from the style of clothing worn by the onlookers, this photograph was taken during the Edwardian era; the type of clothing (including best dresses, young men's straw boaters and ladies' parasols) suggests it is a summer's day. The Duke of Wellington's Halifax Volunteer Battalion made a fine parade in their red tunics, marching up Waring Green on their way to Lane Head recreation ground. Why? The date is Sunday 22 June 1911, and these were the Brighouse celebrations for the Coronation of King George V.

This is a procession float from around 1907 belonging to the Brighouse Cooperative Society. In more modern times the gala float would be more likely to have children from a local organisation on the back – although present-day insurance requirements have made this almost a thing of the past. In 1907 at the Brighouse demonstration parade local traders used the floats to advertise their merchandise whilst raising money for worthy charities.

The Brighouse cemetery chapel was built by S.W. Dyson to the winning design of Peyton & Gray, a firm of architects from Bradford. There was a delay, however, once the work had been started following the news that one of the joiners had gone bankrupt. The chapel was finally completed in 1873 and, after the grounds had been laid out by local landscape gardener Lister Kershaw, the cemetery was formally opened in 1874.

The Lads On Town Tonight (*c.* 1960) – Brighouse teddy boys in Blackpool on a day out. Despite setting off from Brighouse on the train with bright clean faces, on arrival in Blackpool their faces were a blackened grey smoke colour, as they had stuck their heads out of the carriage windows. Those enjoying their day out included Dave Carter, Mick Kelly, Johnny Davis, Johnny Joyce, Graham Greatorex, Mick Green, Barry Darwin, Brian Metterick, Billy Oates, Glyn Ripley and Peter Hirst.

It is difficult to imagine the ferocity of the fire in 1905 which completely destroyed the top floors of the Victoria Mill. The borough fire brigade were able to do little other than prevent it from jumping across the canal and setting another mill alight. Surprisingly, those parts of the mill that remained were renovated and were occupied almost continually by businesses until all the property in this view was demolished. In 1998 J. Sainsbury Ltd opened its new 31,000sq ft supermarket on the site.

Left: Derek Garside proudly standing in his Brighouse & Rastrick Band uniform. Born in 1930 in Brighouse and from a musical family, Derek started playing the cornet at the age of nine, joining the Clifton & Lightcliffe Band in 1942. He joined the Brighouse & Rastrick Band in 1943, and in 1947 he was appointed the principal cornet at the CWS (Manchester) Band, a position he held with distinction for twenty-five years. Many people within the brass band world considered him to be the finest player of his generation.

Below: The St John's Ambulance Brigade Marching Band, many people would say was the finest of its kind. It excelled in almost all the competitions it entered, and when it was marching through the town everyone stood to attention, such was its precision in marching, playing and deportment; a tribute to the young people of the band. This community day parade with the St John's band was on the Smith House estate in 1948.

Having been at Brighouse for over forty years, the waterworks office in Mill Royd Street was closed on Wednesday 31 March 1971, and all the equipment was transferred to the new head office of the Calderdale Water Board at Thrum Hall. The Brighouse staff in this 1971 photograph include Jeff Crawshaw, Ernest Bailey, Eric Wakefield, Frank Norman, Herbert Gilson, Brian Fox, Chris Hirst, Nigel Greenwood, Clem Midgley and Harry Hirst. Missing is Fred Womersley, the engineer in charge.

Brighouse bus station in August 1970. The bus station has been moved around the town to various locations, including the first tram terminus outside the George Hotel and Thornton Square. Owler Ings Road was used as a temporary measure, and then in 1941 the open land on Market Street was used. Ten years later it moved to Back Bonegate, and then to here, in Market Street. With the passage of time it moved again to the present site behind Commercial Street, where it waits for that well-deserved makeover.

AGE 15 YEARS.   WEIGHT 15 STONES.

THE RESULT OF EATING
SUGDEN'S FLOUR,
So when ordering

Ask for SUGDEN'S.
Absolutely the Best.

...mpic Study by Bernari ...uger, Brighouse.

A touch of Edwardian publicity with Tom Castle, who was a hefty lad at only fifteen
years old, weighing in at fifteen stones. This advertisement postcard proudly boasts
he achieved this weight by eating Sugden's Flour – and as the slogan says, '…when
ordering ask for Sugden's, absolutely the best…' Young Tom was regularly seen on
Sugden's demonstration parade floats in those pre-First World War days, but sadly he
died a comparatively young man.

two

Clifton

This Coronation procession, winding its way down Clifton Common in 1911, was a time of great celebration. The first Royal visit to Brighouse had been in 1907, and was considered a disappointment by many people. However, in 1912 King George V and Queen Mary embarked on their successful West Riding tour, which included a visit to Brighouse, following the same route as this procession. Once the Royal party arrived in Brighouse it wound its way to the Gooder Lane entrance of the railway station as the King left to continue his tour.

The Armytage Arms at Clifton takes its name from the Armytage family, who occupied Kirklees Hall from 1565 to around 1986. Here are inside views of the Armytage Arms in the 1950s and early 1960s. The licensee is J.C. Ingleby and the telephone number Brighouse 82, but exactly when this postcard was released can only be estimated. An additional clue is the name Harold Betts, with 'his mighty Hammond electronic organ'; it would appear that he was a regular 'turn'. With dancing every night and music on Sundays, it must have been one of the busiest pubs around.

The brass band at Clifton is said to have started in 1838, but had a difficult time during its early days. Early records show it as being more successful from the 1870s onwards. The members and officials of the band posed for this celebratory photograph in 1920 outside the back of the Armytage Arms – note that the young lads are sitting on the edge of the old bowling green, which today is the car park. In 1932 the band moved to Bailiff Bridge and was renamed the Clifton & Lightcliffe Band, and it is still entertaining audiences today.

Throughout the mayoral year the town's first citizen would be invited to countless events presenting prizes, awards and probably being offered more teas than was good for them. But more importantly they had the opportunity of meeting people, both young and old. This gathering was at the annual bring and buy sale outside Clifton Methodist church during the tenure of Councillor Herbert Prest JP as mayor in 1966 and '67, and he was accompanied by his wife Barbara, as he was throughout his term.

Looking from the bottom of Towngate, Clifton in around 1905, showing a number of properties that have since disappeared. The tall building on the left behind the lamp standard is today the function room of the Black Horse Hotel.

The Brighouse Co-operative Society was started in 1856, and by the end of the nineteenth century it had a large network of branches throughout the old borough. This is the Clifton branch, which opened in 1874 at Horsley Fold just off Towngate (seen here in 1899).

It is hard to imagine that during the 1930s Clifton was considered as a potential site for a new Yorkshire airport. The reason for even considering such a thing was largely due to the successful visits to the area of Sir Alan Cobham and his air show. However, the final decision was that the new upgraded airport would be at the Yeadon Aerodrome. Booking a holiday taxi today to Terminal One at Clifton does not have the same ring to it as Terminal One at Leeds Bradford Airport.

This large gathering outside the Armytage Arms was to herald the visit of Princess Louise, the sixth child of Queen Victoria, who was considered a most appropriate person to be invited to open the new art gallery at Brighouse Library. The visit took place on 22 May 1907, and throughout her trip she stayed at Kirklees Hall with the Armytage family. Here we see part of the crowd waiting eagerly for the Royal procession to come into view, but many did not even get a glance of her and were sadly disappointed.

Dumb. Steeple.

References to this, the 'dumb steeple' at Cooper Bridge, indicate that the phrase meant 'doomed steeple', and this was interpreted to mean that a doomed person had reached a place of safety or sanctuary. Just when this dumb steeple was originally erected no-one seems to know, but no doubt some readers may recall the time when it stood in the middle of the road, rather than in its now more familiar kerbside location. The fields in the background were where the Luddites met and held nocturnal meetings in the early nineteenth century.

On 11 June 1921, a 'Grand Garden Party' was held at Kirklees Hall to raise funds for the Clifton war memorial. The committee chairman was Colonel Sir George Armytage, and Fairless Firth was vice chairman. Some of the other committee members included William Bates, James Beevers, Albert Black, A.M. Campbell, James Fell, Daniel Hunter, Amos Priestley, Ernest Rukin, Joseph Seed, John Sutcliffe, Sam Bottomley, C. Brocklehurst, George Hall, Charles Ingham, Herbert Pinder, Thomas Squire, W.L. Sykes, Allen Turver, E.E. Collins and Fred Gordon (secretary). Note that there were no ladies on this committee.

three

Bailiff Bridge

Square Fold was demolished in 1909 to make way for the new showroom and offices of T.F. Firth, a carpet business which had been in Bailiff Bridge since 1867. It was in these cottages that the first school for the children of mill employees was located, and this was also where the first local Methodists worshipped, before the Ebenezer chapel was built. Surprisingly, it was also the home of an inn – quite a contrasting mix of occupants. Note the Bailiff Bridge Club in the background.

Once Square Fold was demolished, this new building site was one of the first in the area to use pre-cast concrete. The tall mill in the background is Jonathan Stott's North Vale Mill, which was opened in 1872 and is still there today, unlike the majority of Firth's carpet mill buildings. Once Firth's closed, almost all of their mills were demolished and redeveloped – only the 1909 office building remains.

Victoria Road and Wakefield Road in around 1905. The shop front gable end is that of Greenwood's Shaving Salon, which in later years was closed and incorporated into the Punch Bowl Hotel. Behind the Punch Bowl were stabling facilities for travellers who were staying overnight. The limeworks on the left were eventually replaced by extensions to T.F. Firth's carpet mill, but like the rest of the mill these have now been demolished and redeveloped.

The Bailiff Bridge crossroads area formed part of the Crow Nest estate at Lightcliffe. The land for these terraced houses was sold off in 1880, and new terraced houses soon followed. Behind these houses was the village's public well, where local people had to bucket out their everyday water needs. The mills in the background have gone, as have the tramcars in the foreground, but the houses on the horizon (built in 1917) are still sought-after today.

Left: This photograph was taken on 31 July 1911, one of those special days in the history of the village. The occasion was the opening and handing-over of the ornamental drinking fountain by Lady Janet Firth, and this was an opportunity for all the local children to be photographed together. The fountain was a local landmark which stood until 1962, when it was unceremoniously dumped on a council depot – an area that looked somewhat like a tipping area. However, this is a happy memory of that glorious day in Bailiff Bridge.

Below: This horse is standing-by, no doubt waiting for that first drink from the new drinking fountain. This was the largest gathering that had been seen in the village for many years. The generous donation of the fountain was gratefully received by Councillor T.C. Dawson on behalf of the Hipperholme Urban District Council, which administered the village at that time.

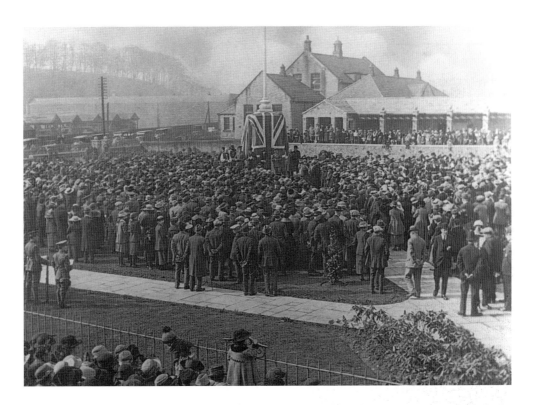

Above: By the end of the First World War, Bailiff Bridge and T.F. Firth's had lost sixty-one of its young men. In memory of those who had lost their lives Sir William and Lady Aykroyd presented the village with a war memorial and garden on 2 April 1921. The unveiling was carried out by Field Marshal Sir William Robertson GCB GCMG KCVO DSO. The service was officiated by the Right Revd George Eden, Lord Bishop of Wakefield. A wooden memorial plaque is also on display in Brighouse Library.

Right: In the summer of 1977 these children from Mayfield Avenue and Mayfield Grove were, like many other children up and down the country, enjoying a street party to commemorate the Silver Jubilee of Queen Elizabeth II.

The Bailiff Bridge Club was opened by Sir Algernon F. Firth on 19 December 1908. It was financed both by him and by his father Thomas Freeman Firth for the benefit of the working men of the village – no mention of ladies in those days. On 27 May 1911, William Aykroyd JP (who was to eventually take over Firth's following the retirement of Sir Algernon Firth) paid for the construction of a new bowling green. This shows the gang who laid out the new green.

Highfield Avenue is a crescent of houses which was built on a greenfield site in 1917. This area had been used extensively for gardening allotments and was locally called 'Garden City'. It was hoped that the new houses would be built only on the outside edge of the crescent, but that was not to be; the allotments were dug up, causing much disappointment. With building work soon following, the once appropriately-named 'Garden City' had gone forever.

four

Lightcliffe

Crow Nest Mansion was occupied and owned by the Walker family from 1687. From 1844 to 1858 it was tenanted to Mr Titus Salt. In 1867 the then owner and occupier of the house, Evan Charles Sutherland-Walker, decided to sell the estate and return to Scotland. Crow Nest was sold for £26,500 to Mr Titus Salt (who was by then Sir Titus Salt) who lived there until his death in 1876. The house has long since disappeared, but in more recent times the site of the property has become the Crow Nest golf club.

Following the death of Sir Titus Salt the estate was purchased by Richard Kershaw, one of Brighouse's most successful nineteenth-century entrepreneurs. He died in 1917 and the estate was put on the market again, being bought by Newton Brooke on behalf of Brooke's Ltd of Hipperholme. This room is the library, seen at the time of the 1917 sale – note the high ceilings.

Evan Charles Sutherland inherited the Crow Nest estate through his aunt in 1854. This was on the condition that he incorporated her name (Walker) into his, which he did. He donated a substantial amount of money towards the building of Lightcliffe Church of England school. Following the sale of the estate in 1867 he and his family went to live at Skibo Castle in Scotland, although they had to leave due to problems in the area and later lived in London, where he died in 1913.

On 3 February 1859, Sutherland-Walker married Alice Sophia Tudor, and they had eight children together. In 1866 they were responsible for removing the old verger's house at the side of Lightcliffe church and moving it to its present location in Till Carr Lane – a fact that is inscribed on a stone tablet at the rear of the building. Such were the complexities of Evan Charles Sutherland-Walker's will that it was 1922 before it was all finally sorted out, nine years after his death.

Left: Sir Titus Salt. Having been a tenant at Crow Nest from 1844 to 1858, he finally bought the property in 1867. It is recorded that he grew tropical fruits in the extensive conservatories. He was also responsible for constructing the lake, which is a problem for golfers these days. On his fiftieth birthday he held a party for all his Saltaire employees, and 3000 turned up – a similar party was held on his seventieth birthday, when 5000 people turned up. He died three years later, in 1876, at Crow Nest.

Below: Coach Road in Lightcliffe was originally the main access to both the Crow Nest and Cliff Hill mansions. The pair of cottages across the road were used as the postal receiving house. The postman Mr Hales would receive the mail at his house and then deliver it on foot around the district, which also included Southowram, as part of his walk to Halifax, where he would collect the return mail.

Wakefield Road was a turnpike road in 1741 – the motorways of their day. The yard on the right was the O'Banks coal-yard, which stood in the grounds of Lightcliffe railway station. It was opened in 1850 and saw a number of distinguished visitors. For example, in 1864 Lord Palmerston came to lay the foundation stone of the Bradford Wool Exchange. At the turn of the century, following a spate of burglaries in Lightcliffe, the offender was caught making his way home to Lancashire using the local train service.

East Street was built on land that was part of the Crow Nest estate. Land from this estate was being sold off from 1867 right through to the turn of the century. Facing these houses were open fields with an almost uninterrupted view across the valley. Between 1949 and 1953 the fields were developed for new social housing, which saw the construction of the Stoney Lane estate. Some readers may well remember when the corner shop there was the Economic Stores.

In January 1995 it was reported that the Lightcliffe Drum and Bugle Corps had sounded its last note, having decided to close down. It had begun life as the Lightcliffe Scout Band some twenty years earlier. During its lifetime the name was changed to the Lightcliffe Kingsmen, and then the Drum and Bugle Corps. One of the band's finest moments came when it took part in the National Championships at Chelsea Football Club. The band decided to finally fold when the membership was down to seven. Here is the band in the successful days of the 1980s.

The top of Stoney Lane looks out onto Wakefield Road and the old Lightcliffe church. Originally built in 1529, the church was rebuilt in 1775 and was eventually demolished in 1969, leaving only the tower as a lasting memory. Behind the cottages on the left is the Sun Inn public house. Prior to 1739 it was known as Mortimer's Farm, but when the road became a turnpike road changing to a coaching inn was obviously considered a better business opportunity. Even in the early twentieth century the inn still had stabling facilities.

Above: Holme House was the home of Sir Algernon Firth, but he was only a tenant. It was originally built in 1820 by the Armytage family, but they left in 1841 when it was purchased by the Ripley family, the founders of the Ripley dyeworks in Bradford. This family retained ownership until 1975, when the property was converted into houses within a house. Visitors who have stayed at the house include Lord Palmerston, Frederick Delius and Herbert Asquith MP, who visited before he became Prime Minister in 1908.

Left: Sir Algernon Firth was the son of Thomas Freeman Firth, who started Firth's Carpet Company at Bailiff Bridge in 1867. Following the death of his father he became one of the managing directors of the company. He and his wife, Lady Gertrude Janet Firth, lived at Holme House in Lightcliffe from 1887 until he retired from the company. They moved to Scriven Park in Knaresborough in around 1921 where he died in 1930.

Longlands was a large stone-built house situated on Leeds Road, and is seen here in 1956. It was originally built in 1904 for Miss E. Watkinson, daughter of Canon Watkinson of Halifax, whose family had strong ties with the Lightcliffe area. The property was later owned by the Standeven family, who had a well-established worsted factory in Halifax. In 1956 the house was owned by West Riding County Council, and it was opened as a residential home for the elderly, with Miss A. Dickinson as the first matron.

It was while the property was owned and occupied by the Standeven family that the celebrated Coley woodcarver Mr Herbert Percy Jackson created thirty different wood panels for the house. This photograph shows the furnished hall and some of his fine panel work.

In 1947 work started on a large new housing estate in Lightcliffe. This aerial view takes you back to those early days, showing where the road network had just been completed on the new Stoney Lane estate. The first house officially handed over to its new tenants was No. 34 Fairless Avenue. That day many distinguished people visited the house before the family could finally settle down in their new modern home

It was not long after the houses in the new Stoney Lane estate were built that new tenants began to form lasting friendships and bond together as a new community. Here we are looking at a partially-built Shirley Grove (a street name with a Brontë connection, perhaps) at the junction with Fairless Avenue, a new street with another literary connection – it was probably named after local author Margaret Fairless Barber (1869-1901), who wrote under the pen name of Michael Fairless.

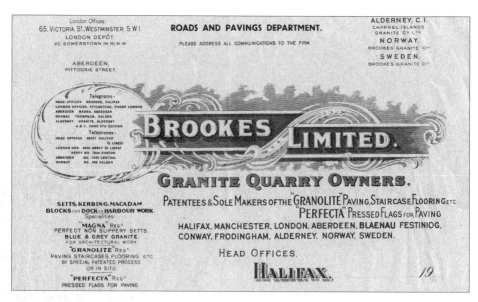

For well over a century the stone industry thrived in Lightcliffe – the firm of Brooke's Ltd began stone quarrying in the mid-nineteenth century and employed generations of men and boys from the immediate locality, and from further afield. After the company patented the first successful 'nonslip' flagstone on 30 March 1898 they never looked back, and diversified into many other areas. After the Second World War the company's fortunes turned and in 1969 Brookes' Ltd ceased to exist. This letterhead gives some indication of how big the company was.

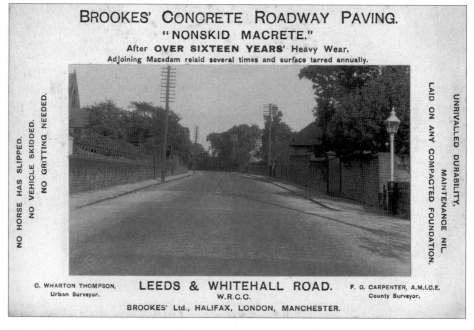

The Leeds and Whitehall Road at the top of Sutherland Road, showing an advertisement for Brooke's concrete road paving. This was just one aspect of the company's diversification, which also included house-building, chemical production and the manufacture of every kind of brick imaginable.

five

Hipperholme

A.E. Northend's tailors, drapers and hosiers shop stood on a corner of Hipperholme crossroads from as early as 1906. The double-fronted shop next door is the grocery business of George Webster & Son, which will be a familiar name to many older readers. The uniformed person is likely to be the postman. The initials embossed onto the corner below the quartered top window are W.H.B. – Walter Henry Bentley, who was in the stone industry and probably either supplied the stone or built the property.

The days of Edwardian elegance – judging by the number of straw boaters and summer frocks these people are taking afternoon tea during the summertime. The location is the Victoria tennis club, which was very close to Victoria Terrace and became known as 'Tennyson Bungalow'. The tennis club was originally formed in 1883. Note the large Brooke's Nonslip Stone Co. premises in the background.

Above: Where did a particular street get its name from? This is a question I am often asked. This row of properties is called Brookeville, and is on Halifax Road. These properties were built by the Brooke's stone company, and made from Brooke's stone. Once the houses were finished they were appropriately named after the family who owned the company. The houses were built in 1911 and, judging from the colour of the stonework, they had not been finished for long when this photograph was taken.

Right: Maynard Percy Andrews MA was the new headmaster of Hipperholme Grammar School in April 1911. In 1912 he joined the Brighouse Territorial Army, and was very quickly promoted to captain. On 14 August 1915 he was in the deep muddy trenches near Ypres, along with his fellow soldiers of the 4th West Ridings. He was killed in action by a German sniper whilst helping a badly-wounded comrade. His act of bravery in helping that comrade later earned him a mention in dispatches.

I am sure many of you will remember your school days, whether they were good or bad. The Hipperholme infant school closed over fifteen years ago, and was later demolished. I am sure these children, some of whom are grandparents now, will look on the vacant site and recall many fond memories, such as this Christmas nativity event in the 1940s – were you one of the three kings?

FENNY COTTAGE

Many people may never have seen Fenny Cottage before. Unless you know where it is the only time you could see it from the main road is from the top deck of a bus. This view is looking from high up in the old brewery on the opposite side of the road. However, even if you do see it, the present-day garden layout is far different to this stylised garden from over ninety years ago.

It is 22 June 1911, and this was the largest gathering ever witnessed at the Hipperholme crossroads. The occasion was the Coronation of King George V. Judging by the coats the crowd are wearing the weather is poor, with the bit of road surface visible looking positively wet.

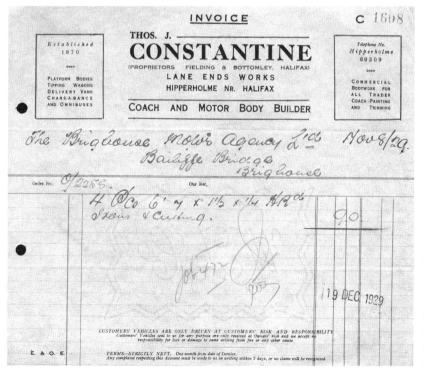

This invoice is to the Brighouse Moor Agency and is dated 8 November 1929. It shows that T.J. Constantine's was actually owned at that time by Fielding & Bottomley of Halifax.

Above left: It was July 1908 when Sir Algernon Firth gave Hipperholme Grammar School its first fives court, which was based on the Winchester Fives pattern. Here are the 'Brighouse House' fives champions from 1911 – C. Stead and H.A. Binns. That original fives court has gone now, replaced by a modern design technology and information technology facility. Appropriately that new classroom is called Room Five.

Above right: The name of Dorothy Stevens has been synonymous with ballet and dance for more years than most people dare to count. This photograph was taken when Dorothy was aged ten. Throughout her distinguished career she has seen and trained countless young people at her studios, and now many of her former students bring their own children for the same respected and excellent tuition.

Right: Thomas J. Constantine started his business in 1870 making bodies for carts and then wagons. This was later extended into delivery vehicles, charabancs and (as the letterhead says) even 'omnibuses'. He was elected to Hipperholme council in 1901, and in 1906 was elected its chairman. His premises were on Leeds Road, in what is now the yard of LCW Truck and Van Hire. It was on that site that the business suffered from a major fire.

CROW NEST

six

Hove Edge

Yew Cottage

Giles House

MR RICHARD KERSHAW

Lower Green

LOT 15
A R P
4 · 0 · 10

LOT
A R
2 · 3

Sheard Green

Upper Green

HOVE EDGE

After legally becoming a part of the Brighouse parish in 1894, steps were immediately taken to build Hove Edge a school. Plans were soon drawn up by local architect George Hepworth and on Sunday 5 May 1895 the new school was opened. On Sundays the new building was used as a mission church. By the end of that year the building had taken the name 'St Chad's mission church and school'. With the opening of the new St Chad's church in 1899, the need for the mission church ceased and the building was used solely as a school.

Here are the trustees of the old Zion Methodist church of 1963. From left to right, back row: T.K. Laycock, Frank Hardy, Peter Green, Norman Hopwood, K. Foreman, D.P. Briggs, R. Wood. Middle row: D.B. Mason, E.A. Leach, D. Rushton, P. Johnson, Revd P. Colquhoun, H. Crowther, G.A. Varley, L. Oates, J. Varley. Front row: Miss S. Tabrah, Mrs Nortcliffe, Miss A.M. Milnes, Mrs Mason, Miss E. Edwards, Mrs Marsden, Mrs Slinger, Mrs Crowther, Mrs Grindrod. Many of these people still have relatives in the community.

Pub trips, summer outings and mystery charabanc trips were just some of the events eagerly anticipated every year by countless organisations. This trip from the 1950s shows the men of the Old Pond Inn about to set off on their coach – what odds would you give that it was a race-day trip?

I am sure many Hove Edge readers will recognise their old branch of the Brighouse Industrial Society, seen here in 1899. It was opened on 25 April 1881 at the corner of Halifax Road and Half House Lane. By the 1960s practically all of the branches had been closed. While some of them were demolished, with the sites being redeveloped, others (like the one shown here) were put to an alternative commercial use.

How many pubs have there been in Hove Edge? I am sure many readers will be able to identify at least two - the Dusty Miller and the Old Pond Inn. But what about the Broad oak Inn (or Broadoak Tavern, as it was sometimes known), which closed in 1935? Here we see a fourth pub, the Joiners Arms, which was closed in 1931 when Hannah Greenwood was the licensee. Today the building is the Hove Edge post office.

The 'Hove Edge Old Folks Annual Treat' is a community event that is sadly missed today. This much-loved event was conceived at a meeting in the Old Pond Inn in 1885, where those attending proposed that there should be an annual get-together for the elderly residents of the community, which should take the form of a tea. The Hove Edge teas were run with military precision by a tireless committee of dedicated people. Here we see some of the folks at the 1980 'Treat', at the Zion chapel.

During the 1970s and '80s the battle was on to develop the old Crow Nest mansion site. The objectors dug in, arguing that if the developers got their way most of Hove Edge, Lightcliffe and parts of Hipperholme would lose their individual identities and would effectively become one huge residential community. The objectors ensured that the main plan never came to fruition, although houses were built on the largest of these green fields.

After the devastating munitions explosion in 1916 at the Low Moor works, the War Office announced that in future only smaller sites would manufacture picric acid. One of the selected sites was at the Brookes' chemical factory in Halifax Road. At 5.30 a.m. on Friday 22 December 1917 there was a massive explosion at the works; two employees were killed outright and a further three died later of their injuries. Here is a group photograph showing some of the munitions workers on a happier occasion.

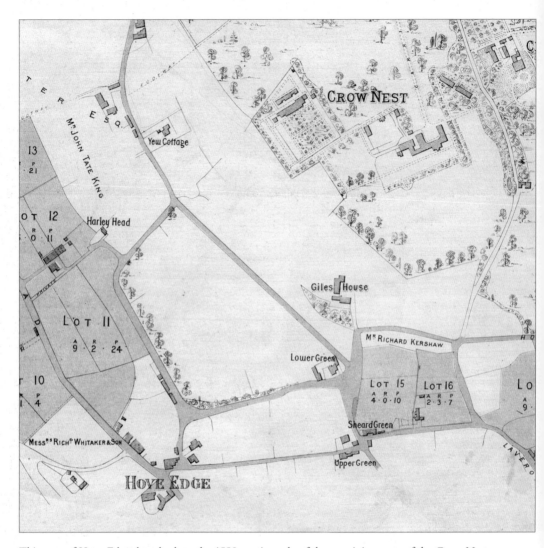

This map of Hove Edge dates back to the 1890 auction sale of the remaining parts of the Crow Nest estate land, which had being progressively sold off after the initial sale in 1867. While there are few buildings on this map, some of them have very interesting histories. The offices of administration for the old Hipperholme-cum-Brighouse township were at Harley Head for a short time, premises which were then used as the equivalent of a town hall. This was a result of the township separating in 1866 into two distinct areas. Yew Cottage, on the same side of the road, does not exist any more; there was also a private girls' school on that site during the nineteenth century. There were few other houses or buildings, although Giles House and Sheard Green are shown. The properties and all the land on this map belonged to the estate. It is clear that if the original Crow Nest sale of 1867 and all the subsequent sales had not taken place, then Hove Edge, Lightcliffe, Hipperholme, Bailiff Bridge, Southowram and parts of Halifax would not exist today as we know them, if at all.

seven

Sunny Vale Pleasure Gardens

It was Joseph and Sarah Bunce who started what many small children simply called 'Sunny Bunce's' in 1880. Half-way down the lane from Hove Edge was (and still is) a giant stone column, and it was over the top of this that pulleys were used to carry tubs to and from the Walterclough pit in the valley bottom.

Initially just a place for nineteenth-century summertime Sunday strollers, Sunny Vale soon developed into what many were calling 'the playground of the north', the Alton Towers of its time. Usually, visitors (even from the local Sunday school or the Oddfellows organisation) had to pre-book their tea. In these buildings were the tea rooms where sandwich-making became almost an art form, and throughout the season ladies would make literally thousands of quartered sandwiches and serve gallons of mineral water to the children.

There were also some unforgettable stage performances from groups of children, including a performance from the 'Rainbow Revels' in 1943. This group includes Muriel Swift, Jessie Earnshaw, Dorothy Waterhouse, Phyllis Gledhill, Connie Hamer, Miss Mildred Crossley (the dancing teacher), Derek Hamer, Pat Wilkinson, Elaine Mallinson, Dorothy Preston, Shirley Lee, Jean Preston, Mary Preston, Muriel Waterhouse, June Thorpe, Jean Midgley, Vera Wilkinson and Joan Earnshaw. One name missing from this group is the late Roy Castle, who appeared regularly with Mildred Crossley's 'Sunny Valians' on the old Sunny Vale wooden stage.

In the early days at Sunny Vale the Alexandra and Victoria lakes were the tops. However, as the years went by visitors wanted more and their expectations had to be catered for. An early attraction to be added was 'water cycling', which was not for the faint hearted, and no ladies of course. Young men would not be seen in anything other than their three-piece suit, Albert chain, a new cap from the local Co-op and, of course, the shiniest boots in town.

The recently discovered Mitchell and Kenyon archive films showed a scene not dissimilar to these, the only moving pictures in existence of Sunny Vale and the donkey rides. All the visiting children wanted a ride on the donkeys. Before the First World War, 100,000 visitors a season would go to the Walterclough Valley.

'Baby Bunce'. In 1917 Sunny Vale had its own miniature railway, which was purchased and added following the closure of Halifax Zoo. The train began its working life on Blackpool sands for the new Blackpool Pleasure Beach Co., but eventually it was moved to Sunny Vale. Today the train is still giving children a lot of fun rides, more than a century after it first ran, only now it is at the Lightwater Valley amusement complex under its original name of 'Little Giant'.

A poster advertising an excursion to Sunny Vale on Saturday 20 June 1931.

Having spoken to many people who, as children, took part in the Sunny Vale experience, I discovered one fairly common and previously unknown piece of information from many of them, namely 'how to get into Bunce's for now't'. This piece of information came mainly from Southowram residents, who could remember quite easily that the free way in was through a hole in the fence and then through the maze. The maze was originally planted in around 1909, but by the 1940s it was in a poor state of repair.

A multi-view postcard with five illustrations, showing activities that would make you the envy of all your friends when they received this postcard back at home. Of course, you could only stay for the day, as there were no facilities to stay overnight, but postcards were much more popular back then, and would even be sent from single days out.

eight

Rastrick

The bottom of Bramston Street in Bridge End has often been described as the gateway up to Rastrick. These major roadworks occurred because new sewer mains were being laid through the town during the early 1960s, an event that caused major disruption for weeks on end. The Rising Sun (one of four pubs in this small area) was demolished in 1913, which explains why the bottom of Bramston Street is so wide today.

A typical corner shop of its era. This was Dixon's shop ('We sell almost everything') in Closes Road at the corner with Thornhill Road. These streets (along with Stoney Hill, Lillands Lane, Firth Street, Thomas Street and George Street) housed a great number of people, in the days when big families were commonplace. Today these properties in Closes Road have all been lost in the mists of time, replaced by the Thornes Park estate.

While today the church takes care of our spiritual needs, in the old days it often took care of our social needs as well. The church still holds many different kinds of events throughout the year. This is the St Matthew's parish church annual garden party in 1966. The Revd. Ian Knox, who was vicar from 1960 to 1977, is addressing the guests and no doubt introducing the mayor, Herbert Prest, and his wife Barbara.

The Rastrick House coach house is all that remains of this old property, although its original entrance lodge does still stand at the end of Field Top Road and Field Lane. The house was originally built by John Clay on some land that he bought from the Fryer family in 1813. It was also the temporary home of a number of evacuees from the Second World War bombing of Coventry in 1941.

The Coronation of King George V in June 1911 was marked by a number of celebrations throughout Brighouse and many of its surrounding communities. One of the most popular events was this ox roasting at Round Hill in Rastrick. The ox took two days to cook, and then there was enough meat to make 3000 sandwiches, using 120 loaves. It was reported in the local newspaper that one person made a comment to the reporter that the beef was 'tender as a chicken!'

While dark clouds were looming over Europe in 1937, other local events were also making news. The first and second teams at New Road Sunday school played in the Huddersfield and District cricket league, and this photograph was taken to celebrate the first team winning both the Lumb Cup and becoming First Division Champions, and the second team becoming the Second Division Champions and winning the Armitage Shield – a unique double. In 1988 the New Road team became the Badger Hill Cricket Club.

RATEPAYERS OF RASTRICK,

DON'T BE GAMMONED
BY WILSON'S COMMITTEE,

BUT SUPPORT MR. DOBSON'S NOMINEES,

as it is most important that he should be supported by a majority in the Local Parliament.

Grave interests are at stake. Mr. Dobson is eminently qualified for the post of Chairman of the Board, being a native, and one of the largest owners of property and employers of labour, as well as a large contributor to the rates of the Township. Naturally his interests and yours are identical.

His scheme for purchasing the Waterworks will land our Township in such prosperity that henceforward we shall have no rates to pay. Ponder this carefully, Fellow Ratepayers! You know well he has shown by his figures that Water only is worth an indefinite sum a year to the Ratepayers.

His calculations are based on the most abstruse research, and his business capabilities are so immense that he ought to lead the Board. Down with the Gas Company! Down with the Water Company! that have done so much mischief to the Township, and return to your old ways. **Candles for ever! Wells for ever!** and waste not your money on street lamps which will not burn!

Fellow Ratepayers, do not be gulled. Put men on to our Local Board who are small ratepayers: they know what burdens they have to bear—men who are not in a large way of business, for they understand details of expenditure. They can give you the benefit of their experience, and know the value of all the necessaries of life, which is so important to the existence of a Local Board.

Don't be humbugged. Wilson promoted both the Gas and Water Companies which have done so much harm. When the Local Board saw the folly of indulging in these useless luxuries, he advised every one to burn gas instead of candles, and to have water in their houses instead of walking to get it from the pure springs at the beginning and end of the day. Consequently property is worth less than it was ten years ago! The population is decreasing rapidly, and soon we shall have streets of empty houses, because no one will live in a house with gas and water in it.

Ponder the position, and Vote accordingly.

A SMALL RATEPAYER.

During the 1880s there was disappointment and disquiet in Rastrick at the workings of the local board, especially in relation to the gas and water companies and claims that they were profiteering. In 1887 the Rastrick Ratepayers Association was reformed, after a lapse of fifteen years. In 1888 the association sponsored six candidates at the local board elections. They were all successful, and this was one of the election posters they were using at the time.

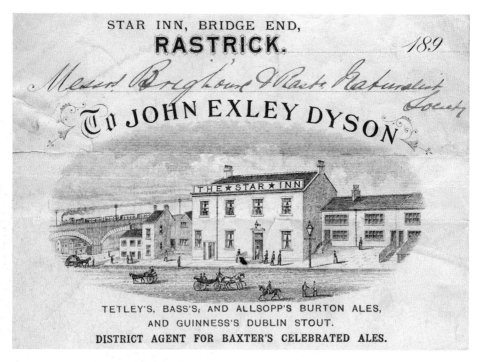

STAR INN, BRIDGE END,
RASTRICK.

189

Messrs Brighouse & Rastr Naturalist Society

To JOHN EXLEY DYSON

THE ★ STAR ★ INN

TETLEY'S, BASS'S, AND ALLSOPP'S BURTON ALES,
AND GUINNESS'S DUBLIN STOUT.
DISTRICT AGENT FOR BAXTER'S CELEBRATED ALES.

Exactly when the Star Inn opened its doors for the first time remains a mystery, but this paid invoice dates back to 21 December 1895, when the licensee was John Exley Dyson. The invoice appears to be for one year's room hire by the Brighouse and Rastrick Naturalist Society, who obviously met at these premises and paid £2 annually for the pleasure of it.

The people of Bridge End once boasted about having four pubs: the Star, which is on the right-hand side (the only one still serving today); the White Lion, which was next door (the only separation being the old 'Star steps', as they were known), which closed in 1908; the Duke of York, which was further along towards the bridge, and which closed in 1927; and the Rising Sun, which was in the middle of Bramston Street, demolished in 1913.

nine

Brookfoot

In 1908 two local businessmen, John Henry Turner and George Wainwright, moved from their premises in River Street in Birds Royd, which by that time were bursting at the seams. They took a business gamble and moved into the empty Camm's five-storey cotton mill at Brookfoot. They were embarking on an expansion programme which could ensure the success of their business, or lead to bankruptcy. We are talking, of course, about the company which adopted the trade name of 'Turnwright's', the Turner and Wainwright Toffee Co.

The name Turnwrights was known to countless First World War soldiers who were away in France. The much-welcomed comfort parcels they received often contained a piece of slab toffee, and the label told them that it was a gift from Brighouse. Here we see the packing room, which was generally staffed by ladies. These premises have had a number of different owners since those days, including Meredith & Drews and Kossett Carpets.

With the Wharf Inn just showing on the left, the Neptune Inn at the bottom of Brookfoot Hill and rows of terraced houses standing alongside the road, Brookfoot was a self-contained community. There were mills up the valley, and the old cotton mill between the canal and the river. You have to wonder where everyone went – little remains of this small, proud community, but in 1905 the place was alive and thriving.

As you pass through Brookfoot today along Elland Road, any sense of the old community has long since faded into a memory. It is difficult to imagine these days that Brookfoot was once a community in its own right, with a school, church and roadside cottages. It could boast enough hostelries to keep all its residents well-refreshed, as well as the daily 'comer's-in' who worked alongside the canal at what became known as 'Brookfoot's inland port'.

St Anne's church at Southowram served the needs of the local communities, but it was felt that the spiritual needs of the growing population of Brookfoot were being neglected. This was rectified with the opening in 1895 of St Peter's mission church, seen here not long after it opened. Eventually numbers in the congregation declined, and it was decided to close the mission in 1959.

The new St Peter's school opened its doors in March 1878, but in 1974 the school was closed down, having been deemed to be in a dangerous condition. I believe this was the last school photograph, taken in July 1973. Perhaps you were one of these students, or even one of the teachers, on that summer's day just over thirty years ago?

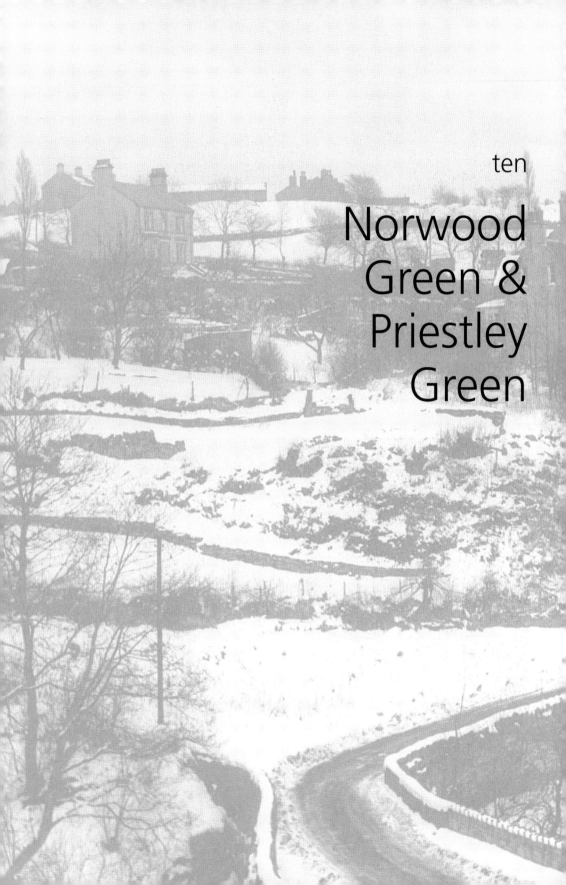

ten

Norwood Green & Priestley Green

Above: This view of Norwood Green Hill is in stark contrast to the same view today. Although most of these quaint old properties still remain, they have now been surrounded by many more modern properties. The Ellis jubilee clock tower still dominates the top of the hill. It was erected in 1897 by Mrs Ephraim Ellis, her two daughters and her son Lewis Ellis, in memory of the late Mr Ellis, and in honour of Queen Victoria's Diamond Jubilee.

Left: Charlotte Oates, the Norwood Green poetess, was born in 1856 in Halifax, but in 1865 she moved to Norwood Green. By the time she was twelve she could write, sing, play the piano and do much of the housework and baking for her mother. Her first published poem was in the *Blackpool Herald* in 1877. Towards the end of her life she published a book of poetry and following her death in 1900, a second volume was published by her brother Arthur in her memory.

An important event for the Norwood Green Good Companions Club. Mrs Joyce Hulme stands poised to cut the club's birthday cake in 1956 while her husband Leslie, who was deputy mayor, looks on. Some of the officials, welfare officers and members of the Companions Club are gathered around.

A rare photograph of Field Head, a small row of cottages which were demolished during the 1950s. Older readers may remember some of the occupants – Mr Lister, who worked on the railways; James Hamilton Smith, who had two of the cottages; Charlie Hawkins; and the unforgettable Phoebe. She was the lady who delivered the milk around the village, and she never missed a round, come hail, rain or shine. These cottages had no running water, just two wells, one for drinking water and one for washing – what a life.

Above: During the First World War many casualties were sent to local military hospitals to recover, including at Boothroyd in Rastrick, or Holroyd House at Priestley Green, where over 900 soldiers passed through over those four years. To this day there is a plaque in the house which was presented for the help that was given to the young injured soldiers during those difficult years.

Left: The military hospital at Priestley Green was run by the commandant, Lady Gertrude Janet Firth of Holme House in Lightcliffe. She was later mentioned in dispatches for the work she and her team had diligently carried out at Holroyd House. She was also a prominent supporter of the Young Helpers League, and carried out many tasks of a philanthropic nature in Bailiff Bridge.

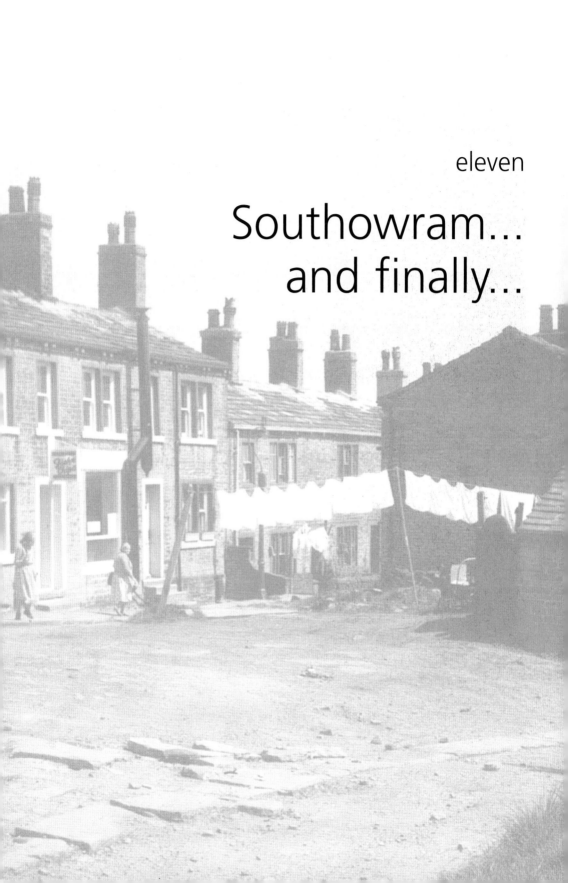

eleven

Southowram...
and finally...

The avid local postcard collector cannot have failed to notice that there are few old picture postcards of Southowram. This is one of the small number of multi-view postcards still to be found. The image in the top left-hand corner is of Towngate; in the top right is an image of Bank Top; in the bottom left is St Anne's-in-the-Grove church; in the bottom right is Higgin Lane; and in the centre, we are looking up Cain Lane towards the Shoulder of Mutton public house. It was only in 1913 that the streets in this hilltop community received the benefit of street lamps.

Southowram did not avoid the demolition men's hammers. This collection of old cottages was called New Road and all of these buildings were swept aside, once again in the name of progress. It is interesting to note that the middle house in the row of terraced houses on the left has a sign outside indicating that it was a fish and chip shop, but it does not say who the owner was – perhaps you can remember who the owners were?

It has been estimated that before the First World War there were some 15,000 brass bands in this country. Southowram Prize Band started in 1901, and for a time it did well in local contests and performed many concerts in the Southowram, Halifax and Brighouse areas. It even played in the National Contest in London, but missed out on the prizes. By the 1930s the band was in difficulty, and in 1938 Arthur Green, the secretary, announced that the band had folded through lack of interest.

The 'Ba Gum, Who Wad'a'Thowt It' Inn in Walterclough Lane was licensed from the 1860s. It went through a period of difficulty and on one occasion had a brush with the law for after-hours drinking. Its demise finally came on 27 December 1933 when it stopped selling beer, but it did continue serving cups of tea for some time as a café. In 1941 the old building was finally demolished, with most of the old stone roof slates going to help rebuild some of the houses bombed in the Blitz around Coventry.

And finally…

I hope you have enjoyed this book, and that it has rekindled your own memories of Brighouse and its surrounding communities. We have to make progress and things do have to change, but sadly they don't always change for the better. The so-called 'good old days' are nice to look back on, but in many ways they are best left confined to the history books, only given an airing every now and again, when that feeling of nostalgia returns as we all get older.

Opposite above: On 7 July 1957 the mayor Alderman Harry Edwards and his wife the mayoress visited the Southowram 'Old Folks Treat'. This annual event attracted 200 guests for tea, and a further sixty-five guests were unable to attend and had their tea delivered to them. The mayor was welcomed by the president of the tea committee Revd. Philip Burton, the vicar of Southowram. This photograph shows the mayor and mayoress, Mr Burton, members of the committee and some of the guests.

Opposite below: The Southowram tramway was formally opened on 19 September 1901. Three tramcars made that first journey from Halifax up to the hilltop community at Southowram. The dignitaries were all on the first tramcar, the Southowram Subscription Band were on the second and the first passengers were on the third – no doubt this was the first and last occasion that they were able to travel free-of-charge. After the ceremony was over everyone adjourned to the Sion congregational schoolroom for refreshments.

Below: Since that day Brighouse and its surrounding communities have changed significantly. This is an aerial photograph of the town, taken in 1990. Fears in the 1970s that the town centre would only have two shops (Hillards and the Co-op) proved unfounded. Brighouse has a number of large shops, including Wilkinson's, Tesco and of course Sainsbury's, but it also has a wealth of smaller local shops, and it is these establishments and their familiar owners and staff that many of us in the area will continue to support.

The *Brighouse Echo* has reported on local matters since it became our local newspaper on 24 June 1887, under the editorship of its owner John Hartley. It has reported on many events in the community's history, some sad and many happy. It has always been there whenever local people have turned out in great numbers, so I will close this book with one of their images, taken at the Brighouse gala in Wellholme Park, on 28 June 1992.

Opposite above: A lot has changed since this picture was drawn, in the days when most local people were only just moving from an agricultural workplace to an industrial one. The picture is taken from a print of Brighouse dated 1841, and is looking from approximately where New Street in Clifton is today. (From Tate's *Views of Manchester to Leeds Railway*, 1845)

Opposite below: On 30 September 1893, a great day in the history of Brighouse, the town clerk James Parkinson reads out the Charter of Incorporation outside the town hall. The first meeting at which it was proposed that Brighouse should submit a proposal to apply for a charter was in 1890. The following year a meeting was held at the town hall where it was formally proposed. In February 1892 consultation with the public took place, and then in August 1893 came the announcement that a charter had been granted.

Other local titles published by Tempus

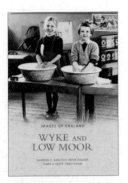

Wyke and Low Moor
MAUREEN BARSTOW, PETER WALKER, MARY AND GEOFF TWENTYMAN

This collection of over 200 archive photographs highlights some of the changes that have taken place in and around the villages of Wyke and Low Moor, which still bear the scars of Bradford's industrial past. Perhaps the most prestigious iron foundry in the area was that of the Low Moor Company, which dominated the region for over 150 years. Accompanied by supporting text, this pictorial history looks back on the area's industrial past and its close-knit communities.

0 7524 3514 0

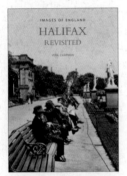

Halifax Revisited
VERA CHAPMAN

This collection of over 200 images illustrates the history of Halifax from around the mid-eighteenth century. Characterised by steep slopes and deep valleys, the district has an industrial past of woollen mills powered by water wheels and steam, and of canals and railways. The town today reflects the changes wrought by the Victorians, who created broad streets and fine buildings. Each image is accompanied by informative captions, providing a nostalgic history of Halifax.

0 7524 3047 5

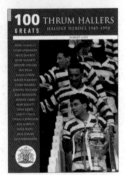

Thrum Hallers: 100 Halifax Greats 1945-1998
ROBERT GATE

Halifax played their last first-team game at Thrum Hall on 22 March 1998. This book is a tribute to 100 notable Thrum Hallers – all from the post Second World War period – who have left generations of followers with indelible memories of stupendous and grim games, famous victories and infamous defeats. Those who saw the deeds of these blue-and-white giants of the game will not forget them.

0 7524 3211 7

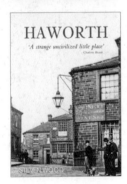

Haworth: 'A strange uncivilized little place'
STEVEN WOOD

The picturesque village of Haworth in West Yorkshire is known worldwide for its association with the Brontë family, who had their home here (the quote in the title is Charlotte Brontë's). This book traces the history of the village, looking at its former farming, textile and stone quarrying industries, its houses, shops and inns, churches, reservoirs and gasworks, and explores some less well-known aspects of the Brontës' connections with Haworth.

0 7524 3508 6

If you are interested in purchasing other books published by Tempus, or in case you have difficulty finding any Tempus books in your local bookshop, you can also place orders directly through our website

www.tempus-publishing.com